THE SEA OTTER

Alvin, Virginia, and Robert Silverstein

THE MILLBROOK PRESS · BROOKFIELD, CONNECTICUT

Cover photograph courtesy © Richard A. Bucich
Photographs courtesy of © Richard A. Bucich: pp. 6, 10, 11, 15, 21, 24,
29, 31, 33, 42; Animals Animals: pp. 12 (Henry Ausloos), 26 (John Gerlach);
Jerry Loomis: p. 18 (both); Peter Arnold, Inc.: p. 23 (Fred Bavendam); Culver
Pictures: p. 36; Willi Baum, courtesy Fort Ross Interpretive Association: p. 39;
Glenn Allen: p. 47; Monterey Bay Aquarium: p. 50; Bettmann: p. 54.
Map by Joe LeMonnier

Library of Congress Cataloging-in-Publication Data
Silverstein, Alvin.
The sea otter / Alvin, Virginia, and Robert Silverstein.
p.   cm. — (Endangered in America)
Includes bibliographical references (p.   ) and index.
ISBN 1-56294-418-5 (lib. bdg.)
Summary: This book presents a wealth of
information about sea otters and
efforts to save them.
1. Sea otter—Pacific Coast (U.S.)—Juvenile literature. 2. Endangered species—
Pacific Coast (U.S.)—Juvenile literature. [1. Sea otter.   2. Otters.   3. Endan-
gered species.] I. Silverstein, Virginia B.   II. Silverstein, Robert A.   III. Title.
IV. Series: Silverstein, Alvin. Endangered in America.
QL737.C25S55   1995   599.74′447—dc20   94-17998   CIP   AC

Published by The Millbrook Press, Inc.
2 Old New Milford Road, Brookfield, Connecticut 06804

CONTENTS

THE SEA OTTER

The sea otter's appeal is hard to resist.

TEDDY BEAR OF THE SEA

People come from all around the world to watch sea otters floating on their backs off the coast of central California. People enjoy the sight of these otters because they seem so playful and affectionate. They are also very clever. Sea otters are one of only a few kinds of animals besides humans and chimpanzees that use tools.

Not everybody loves sea otters, though. In fact, by the beginning of this century, some people had nearly caused these sea animals to become extinct. For nearly two centuries hunters had killed sea otters for their thick, soft fur. By the time laws were passed to protect sea otters, there were almost none left!

Strict laws and concerned people helped sea otters to make a comeback. Their numbers grew until they were no longer endangered. But then some people thought there were too many sea otters. These animals have big appetites and, when feeding, were competing with people who made their living from fishing. Angry fishermen illegally killed sea otters that spread into favorite fishing areas. Even more were killed accidentally when they became tangled in fishing nets.

But this is not the only way that people endanger sea otters. Pollution is threatening many types of marine life. These days, oil spills are the biggest danger. Sea otters cannot survive when their thick fur is covered with oil. In 1989 the biggest oil spill in U.S. history killed thousands of sea otters in Alaska. But many were saved, too, when caring people came to Alaska to clean and care for sea otters injured by the oil.

There are many kinds of otters around the world. Some of them are declining in number because people are taking away the places where the otters live, using them for farms, homes, or industry. Other kinds are threatened by pollution and hunting.

In the 1970s and 1980s people began to worry about the environment and wildlife of the world. This concern is helping to shape the way people see our planet in the 1990s. As more people become concerned, there is a greater chance that animals like sea otters, which were nearly driven to extinction, will be protected for future generations to see and enjoy.

THE SEA OTTER

Sea otters are mammals. Like other mammals, they are warm-blooded, their bodies are covered with fur, and mother sea otters nurse their pups with milk.

Sea otters are carnivores like dogs and cats, which means they are meat eaters. They belong to the weasel family, *Mustelidae*, which includes badgers, weasels, minks, polecats, pine martens, skunks, and about a dozen species, or types, of otters. Most mustelids have scent glands that produce a strong smell. (The skunk, of course, is the most famous stinker of them all!)

The sea otter's scientific name is *Enhydra lutris*. *Lutris* comes from Latin for otter, and *Enhydra lutris* means "otter that lives in the water." All otters live near water, but most otters spend a lot of time on land. Sea otters and South American marine otters (sometimes called sea cats), however, spend nearly all of their lives in the ocean.

Some scientists divide sea otters into three subspecies: the northern sea otter, often called the Alaskan sea otter (*Enhydra lutris lutris*); the southern sea otter, which is often called the California sea otter (*Enhydra*

In a rare moment out of water, this southern sea otter shows the long, streamlined body and thick, tapering tail typical of its kind.

lutris nereis); and the Russian sea otter (*Enhydra lutris gracilis*). Northern and southern sea otters have slightly different behaviors and slightly different bone structures.

WHAT DO SEA OTTERS LOOK LIKE?

Sea otters have a streamlined appearance. They have a small round head, a long heavy body, and a thick, tapering tail that is flat on the bottom. Their eyes are dark, and their noses flat and diamond-shaped. Little pointed ears close when a sea otter dives underwater. The sea otter's whiskers, 4 inches (10 centimeters) long, point downward to act like feelers, helping the animal to find food as it swims along the bottom of the sea.

A sea otter's front paws look like mittens, but they are actually very useful hands. The backs of its front paws are covered with fur, but the palms have tough pads that help the otter to grip prey better. Its claws are retractable like those of a cat. The otter uses them to comb its fur and to snatch up clams from the sea bottom or mussels from a reef.

The sea otter's hind feet are very different from its front paws. They are wide with long webbed toes, forming large flippers for swimming.

A sea otter's clawed front paws are good at grasping prey.
Its webbed hind feet are excellent flippers for swimming.

River Otter
or Sea Otter?

The European river otter is sleek and graceful in and out of the water.

SEA OTTERS are marine mammals; river otters are not. And yet, river otters can sometimes be found swimming and playing in the ocean, where rivers meet the sea. Why aren't they true marine mammals?

River otters and other animals such as beavers find protection and food in water. But they come onto land to have their young. They also must have fresh water. A sea otter doesn't have to drink fresh water; it can drink seawater. And it can live its entire life without ever leaving the sea.

River otters also look quite different from sea otters. They are smaller and much slimmer. A river otter's fur is shorter, too. Unlike sea otters, which are very clumsy on land, river otters can move around very quickly.

The average male southern sea otter is a little more than 4 feet (1.2 meters) long, including a tail about 12 inches (30 centimeters) long. He weighs about 65 pounds (30 kilograms). The average female is a little shorter and weighs about 45 pounds (20 kilograms). Northern sea otters are generally somewhat larger.

An otter's fur is brown to almost black. The underside is often lighter. Pups are born with shaggier, yellowish fur. Often a gray or white face is a sign that an otter is an older adult. But some pups have very light faces, too.

REAL WATER MAMMALS

Sea otters spend most of their time at the ocean surface, lying on their backs. To move around, they usually float on their backs while they paddle with their flippers or move their tails from side to side. Sometimes they swim on their stomachs or stand upright in the water. But mostly, they turn over only when they dive underwater.

Sea otters breathe air like all mammals. But they have to dive to the ocean bottom to find food. Their bodies are well adapted for such diving. Their ears and nostrils close, and their lungs are more than twice as large as those of similar-sized land animals. They can stay underwater for about a minute to a minute and a half, and up to five minutes in an emergency!

Sea otters swim well underwater. The animal's tail, its large webbed feet, and the end of its body sweep up and down at the same time to swoop to the bottom. On land, sea otters move slowly and clumsily, like sea lions.

PROTECTION FROM THE COLD

Like other mammals, sea otters are warm-blooded. The temperature inside their bodies is around 99 to 100 degrees Fahrenheit (about 37 degrees Celsius), no matter what the temperature is around them. Other sea mammals, such as seals, porpoises, and whales, have blubber, a special layer of fat under their skin, to help keep them warm. The blubber acts like insulation to keep body heat from escaping. But sea otters don't have blubber. Their bodies have to work hard to keep their internal temperature constant. And their thick fur keeps their skin from getting wet, which helps prevent heat from being lost.

Sea otters have the thickest fur of any animal. In every square inch there are between 600,000 and one million hairs (more than 100,000 per square centimeter). All together, 800 million hairs cover the average sea otter. To give you an idea of how hairy a sea otter is, there are only an average of 100,000 hairs on a human head!

A sea otter's coat is made up of two layers of fur. The outside layer consists of long guard hairs, which are dark or pale brown. The undercoat is soft and thick, made up of shorter silvery hairs. Pockets of warm air are trapped in the underlayer. This layer of air close to the skin provides the same protection as blubber. The blanket of fur and air acts as a shield against the chill of the water and wind. The layer of air bubbles in the fur also helps the otter to float.

KEEPING CLEAN

Sea otters spend about two and a half hours each day grooming themselves. That time is well spent. When the otter's fur is dirty, it sticks together in clumps so that it cannot trap pockets of air. Without this layer of air bubbles, the skin becomes wet, and the animal becomes chilled.

A sea otter grooms itself on and off all day, but especially after eating. First it rubs its body with its front paws. Then it somersaults forward, rolling over and over to wash away bits of food. After shaking the water

A sea otter grooms its fur.

from its body, the otter licks its fur while it uses its front paws to rub, scrub, and squeeze out water and scratch or comb the fur from head to tail. A sea otter's fur fits very loosely, so the otter can pull on the fur or twist to reach every part of its body. Finally, when it is clean, the sea otter blows warmed air through its nose into its fur.

REGULATING TEMPERATURE

Only the palms of sea otters' front paws, their ears, nose, lips, and the toe pads on their flippers are not protected by heat-holding fur. Even the soles of their hind feet are covered with fur. Holding their unprotected front paws up while they rest keeps the paws dry and helps to save heat.

Sea otters' thick fur helps keep them warm in cold weather, but it can sometimes be a problem. After hard exercise, otters could become overheated in warmer water. But they have effective ways of getting rid of extra heat, too. Special blood vessels just under the skin in the sea otter's feet fill with blood when the otter is overheated, bringing heat to the surface where it can be carried away in the water.

THE SEA OTTERS' WORLD

Sea otters were once found on coasts and islands in much of the north Pacific, from the Baja Peninsula in Mexico up through California, Oregon, Washington, Canada, Alaska, across the Aleutian Islands, the Russian Commander Islands, the Kuril Islands, and along the coast of Japan.

By the beginning of this century, though, only a few scattered groups were left. Today, sea otters can be found over more of their former range, but they haven't recovered nearly as well in some areas as in others.

SEA OTTER HABITAT

The place where an animal lives is called its habitat. Habitats suitable for sea otters are very limited. Since they must dive down to the bottom of the sea to find food, the water cannot be too deep. Sea otters usually live where the water is about 50 to 75 feet (15 to 23 meters) deep. They have to make the trip to the bottom of the sea, find some food, and come back up to the surface in thirty to ninety seconds. The less time they have to

Above: Long strands
of kelp stretch up
toward the sunlit
water surface. Left:
A purple sea urchin
makes a fine meal
for a sea otter.

spend swimming to the bottom and back, the more time they can spend finding food.

The ideal sea otter habitat is an area in which the otters will be protected from harsh winds and other severe weather conditions. Islands, rocks, reefs, and underwater kelp forests are some of the barriers that help calm the waters where sea otters live, keeping them from being dashed against the shore in rough weather.

Kelp is a type of seaweed that is anchored to the bottom of the sea. It reaches up as much as 150 feet (about 46 meters) to the surface, held up by balloonlike, air-filled bladders that float among long stems and leafy blades. The kelp forests in the northern Pacific make up an *ecosystem* in which many different life-forms live together in a delicate balance. Each animal and plant plays an important role in the ecosystem.

The sea otter is considered a *keystone species* in the kelp ecosystem. Scientists can tell how well the ecosystem is doing by seeing how well the sea otters there are faring. Seventy-five years ago, when sea otters were nearly extinct, the kelp forests along the California coast had also greatly decreased. As the number of sea otters has slowly grown, the California coast has also been changing—kelp forests are much thicker.

How does the sea otter play such an important role in the kelp ecosystem? One of the animals that live in the kelp forest is the sea urchin. Sea urchins look like living pincushions, 7 inches (about 18 centimeters) wide. They have round, purple, red, green, or white shells that are protected by long pointy spines. Sea urchins feed on kelp. If nothing preyed on the sea urchins, they would keep on eating until the entire kelp forest was gone. A large shellfish called an abalone also eats kelp. Sea otters eat both of these animals, thus helping to preserve the kelp forests.

Kelp forests provide camouflage for sea otters. Bull kelp is similar to the fur of a sea otter in color. Its brown bladders that float at the surface are much the same size as an otter's head. From a distance it is very hard to tell which floating objects are otters and which are kelp.

In California, sea otters may spend their whole lives in the water, eating, sleeping, grooming themselves, and playing as they float above the kelp forest. But when Spanish explorers first came to California, they saw many sea otters resting on the shore. After two centuries of being killed for their fur, California sea otters adapted to avoid coming out on land. Northern sea otters, which live farther from people, sometimes come ashore. Winter storms are worse in the north, and the water is much colder, so the sea otters may need to find shelter on shore at night or during storms.

A BIG APPETITE

Sea otters have to eat a lot of food to supply the energy their bodies need to keep warm. They can eat about 10 to 15 pounds (5 to 7 kilograms) of food each day—one quarter of their weight! If a 60-pound (27-kilogram) boy or girl ate like a 60-pound sea otter, he or she would need to eat sixty quarter-pound hamburgers each day! So it's not surprising that sea otters spend about one quarter of their lives gathering and eating food.

Other marine mammals, such as whales and dolphins, catch food with their mouths while swimming through the water. But sea otters use their paws to catch food, and they bring it to the surface to eat.

Sea otters prefer shellfish, but their diet varies, depending on where they live and what prey is available. Northern sea otters in the Aleutian Islands eat up to fifty percent fish. Southern sea otters choose their meals from more than forty different marine animals, but almost no fish. Like people, individual sea otters have their own personal favorite foods, too.

A female sea otter nibbles on a crab as her pup floats nearby.

Barnacles, kelp crabs, and turban snails can be found on kelp just below the surface of the water. Deeper down, there are octopuses, squid, and rockfish. At the ocean bottom sea otters find their favorite foods: abalone, sea urchins, and clams, as well as scallops, sea cucumbers, marine worms, starfish, limpets, chitons, and anemones. The strangest prey of all are found in Monterey Bay. Small octopuses in the area hide in beer and soft-drink cans that people have thrown into the water. Sea otters may rip open the cans with their teeth and feast on canned octopus.

Most of the sea otter's prey move very slowly or not at all. The sea otter simply picks them up and carries them to the surface. Limpets and chitons cling to rocks and may have to be pried off with teeth or tugged.

Abalone, which grow up to 10 inches (about 25 centimeters) across, have a thick shell that can keep most predators away. These shellfish can hold themselves down with a force equal to four thousand times their own weight! Humans who harvest abalone must dive down and use a crowbar to pry them up. Sea otters use a tool to hunt abalone, too. They hold a stone the size of a softball between both paws, and use it to hammer the shell. Then they swim up to get some air and come back down to hammer again. They may have to make several dives before the abalone loosens its grip. California sea otters prefer abalone, but these shellfish make up only a small portion of their diet.

DIVING FOR LUNCH

When it is ready to dive, a sea otter takes a deep breath of air and rolls forward into the water. It holds its front paws across its chest as it moves its body up and down to propel itself forward.

The openings to the otter's ears and nose close when it dives, so it cannot smell or hear its prey when underwater. Otters can see underwater better than humans. But the water down at the bottom of the sea may be dark or murky, so sea otters have to rely mostly on their sense of touch.

When it gets to the bottom, a sea otter holds its head back as it pats the ground and rocks with its front paws and reaches into cracks and crevices. The sea otter may grab urchins off the ocean floor, or pry mussels off rocks. It tucks them away in loose folds of skin that extend out

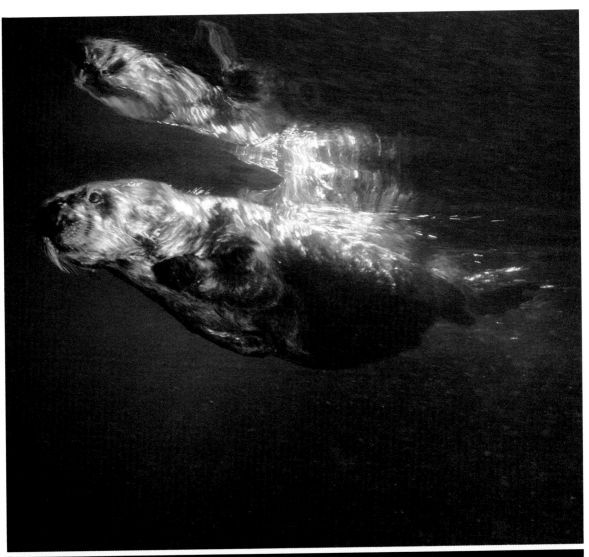

Clumsy on land, the sea otter is an excellent underwater swimmer.

from its chest and under each arm to form a pouch, like a built-in shopping bag. The sea otter's sensitive whiskers may feel crabs or snails hidden in the murky water in the thick seaweed mats.

DINING SEA-OTTER STYLE

When the otter returns to the surface, it eats what it has caught. Lying on its back, it uses its chest as a dining table. Small urchins and mollusks are popped right into its mouth. Half of its thirty-two teeth are strong and flat, perfect for crushing hard shells. But larger sea urchins, mussels, crabs, and clams are broken up into smaller pieces first.

This otter has placed a rock on its chest and is using it to crack open a tasty clam.

The otter uses its eyeteeth to wedge open shells and scrape out the meat. (Sharp claws can also help with this.) But some shells are just too hard to open. That doesn't faze a sea otter. While at the ocean floor it scoops up a rock and carries it to the surface. The otter places the rock on its chest and bangs a clam against the rock until it breaks open.

After the otter has eaten everything it caught, it brushes the bits and pieces of shell off its chest and dives down for some more food. For more than an hour the otter may dive, collect food, bring it up to the surface to eat, then dive, collect, and eat, again and again.

Sea otters gather in groups called rafts.

THE LIFE OF A SEA OTTER

Sea otters may spend their lives in the water, but scientists have been able to learn a lot about them. They are not shy or secretive, like some wild animals. People can observe them from boats or the nearby coast.

Sea otters are usually found floating together in groups called rafts. (When seen from above, the closely packed group looks like a raft.) Sometimes only three or four otters raft together; or there may be several hundred. The most anyone has ever seen was a raft of two thousand sea otters.

Male sea otters usually form their own rafts, away from the females. After a pup is born, the mother raises it herself, without any help from the father. A mother sea otter and her pup form a very close bond. Even though there are many otters floating nearby, the mother and her pup do not interact with the others very much. Pups play with other nearby pups, though, each chasing the others through the waves. The pups may climb over other adults resting nearby, too, until they are scolded by their mothers.

Some animals that live together in groups depend on one another and cooperate in getting food, grooming, and defending the group from enemies. A raft of sea otters is not really a social community of this kind. Sea otters live in groups simply because an area is good for finding food.

TERRITORY

Sea otters usually stay within a certain area or range to rest and hunt. Some types of animals defend their range from other animals of the same species. Sea otters do not normally defend their ranges from neighboring sea otters, although the ranges may overlap. There are some exceptions, however. Some male sea otters defend their territory, chasing other males away. These territorial males have an advantage—first choice for mating with the females in their territory.

OTTER COMMUNICATION

Sea otters make lots of different sounds to communicate. A baby cries when it is left alone. It makes a shrill "wee" sound like a young gull. When sea otters are frustrated or upset they whistle or whine. They hiss or growl when they want to threaten an intruder. They "coo" when they court, and the mother also coos when she grooms her pup's fur with her teeth and claws. Sea otters make grunting sounds when they are content, such as when they are enjoying their food.

Body language is also used to communicate. Sea otters may greet each other by moving their heads from side to side. The pups cling to their mothers or other young otters when they are afraid.

A sea otter pup snuggles safely on its mother's chest.

REPRODUCTION

In Alaska and in the Aleutian chain, most pups are born in the early spring. The water is very rough in the winter there, and it would be hard for a newborn baby to survive. In California, pups are born all year round, but most are seen between January and March. These young pups grow during the season when food is most available.

When a male is ready to mate, he cruises around a female raft. If he finds a female that is ready, he may sniff at her and rub her fur. If she isn't interested, she pushes him away with her front paws or her flippers. If she is interested, she and the male roll over and swim and dive after each other.

It is hard to tell when a female is pregnant because her fur fits so loosely. A single pup is usually born four to six months after mating. Other types of otters have larger litters. A mother sea otter must give lots of attention to her pup, so she cannot raise more than one at a time.

Sea otter pups are usually born in the water. The female rolls forward, somersaulting in the water again and again, until she comes up with the pup in her mouth. A newborn pup weighs 3 to 5 pounds (about 1 to 2 kilograms) and is about a foot and a half (0.5 meter) long.

In the wild, sea otters may live to be fifteen to twenty years of age. Females can have pups when they are about three to four years old. California sea otters usually breed every year, but the northern sea otters in Alaska may have pups only every other year.

CARING FOR THE YOUNG

When a pup is born, the mother places it on one of her nipples. Keeping it snuggled on her chest, she cleans and grooms its fur until it is dry and fluffy. When the baby's woolly coat is cleaned and full of air bubbles, it can float by itself, but it hardly ever gets a chance. Most of the first two weeks are spent sleeping on its mother's chest. After a few weeks the pup will crawl around, using its mother's body as a playpen.

During the first few months, a sea otter pup depends on its mother for everything. She feeds it and grooms its fur carefully to keep it from

Mother and pup share a clam.

becoming chilled. Only when she dives for food or grooms herself does she place her pup onto the water.

Other animals leave their young in a nest or a burrow when they hunt for food. But a sea otter mother has no hiding place in which to leave her pup when she dives for food underwater. So she may wrap strands of kelp across the baby to keep it from floating away, and she never leaves it for more than a few minutes at a time. When she is finished feeding or grooming, she may rise out of the water beneath the pup so that it is once again resting on her chest. Or she may pick it up out of the water using her front paws and her teeth.

California sea otter pups drink their mother's milk for six to eight months, and Alaskan pups for four to twelve months. At one to two months of age, the pup can start to eat solid food caught by the mother. Slowly, the pup learns from its mother how to catch its own food.

First the mother gives her pup swimming lessons. While it is sitting on her chest, she sinks down into the water, leaving the pup to float by itself. Its shaggy fur prevents it from sinking. Next, it has to learn how to dive. When the mother dives down for food, the young pup tries to dive into the water too, but its fur, at first, has too much air trapped inside. Then, at ten to twelve weeks, the pup's woolly fur is slowly replaced by its adult coat. And as it practices, the pup is able to dive deeper and deeper. Soon it is able to both groom itself and dive to the bottom with its mother.

A mother sea otter lets the pup ride on her belly long after it can swim on its own back like an adult. When it becomes too big to climb onto her chest, it rests sideways, forming a T. Or it may float beside her, holding on so that it doesn't float away.

As the pup gets a little older, it is full of energy. (In captivity, playful sea otter pups take out bolts, lift heavy grates, and untie bootlaces.) Slowly the pup becomes more independent. When it is about six months to a year old, the pup begins to get restless. This restlessness soon outweighs the strong bond it had developed with its mother, and the pup sets off on its own. A young male may travel more than 50 miles (80 kilometers) to join a group of other young males, but females usually stay within 5 miles (about 8 kilometers) of where they were born.

SEA OTTER ENEMIES

Sea otters do not have very many natural enemies. Some animals are more of a nuisance than a threat. Eagles and gulls will sometimes swoop down and snatch food from otters, for example.

In the Aleutians, during nesting season, eagle mothers may snatch sea otter pups from the water to feed their new hatchlings. Usually it is a very young pup, because an eagle cannot lift a large otter.

Scientists are not sure whether or not sharks eat sea otters. Sea otters are sometimes killed by sharks, but they may be cast aside when the shark discovers they are not seals, which it prefers. Some wounded sea otters may escape after a shark attack by returning to the kelp bed, where the sharks are reluctant to follow.

Diseases and severe weather conditions have always been dangers that sea otters faced. But starting a few hundred years ago, sea otters met an even more dangerous enemy that nearly drove them to extinction: people.

A gull tries to steal an otter's meal.

THE GREAT FUR HUNT

People have hunted sea otters for food and have worn their furs for thousands of years. Archaeological evidence has shown that native Californians hunted sea otters more than three thousand years ago. Aleuts living on the Aleutian Islands may have hunted sea otters thousands of years before that. But sea otters were only hunted in moderation until the eighteenth century, when they began to be hunted in great numbers. In the 1700s and 1800s sea otter fur was one of the most valuable furs. Hunters came to the North Pacific from all around the world to kill sea otters. It is believed that in less than two centuries, about one million sea otters were killed for their furs.

The story of this great fur hunt began in Siberia. Early eighteenth-century Russian hunters ventured out in springtime to the Kuril Islands, south of the Kamchatka Peninsula in Siberia, to hunt sea otters, which they called Kamchatka sea beavers. They sold the furs to wealthy Chinese who desired them for robes and capes. Until the 1740s sea otter furs were very rare. Then, completely by accident, a rich new source of sea otters was discovered.

DISCOVERIES AND GREED

The Russian czar had sent a Danish navigator named Vitus Bering to find out whether or not America and Asia were joined by land. Bering found that the continents were separated by water, but he discovered the Aleutian and Commander islands between the two continents. On his second voyage to the North Pacific in 1741, Bering and his crew were shipwrecked off one of the Commander Islands, which was later named Bering Island.

Captain Bering and many of his crew starved in the island's freezing cold winter. But one of the survivors, a German scientist named Georg Wilhelm Steller, led a search across the uninhabited island for edible plants and animals. He found sea otters resting on the beaches. These gentle creatures were unafraid of the crewmen—and so were easily killed, providing food and warm furs.

During the long winter, the surviving crewmen gambled to keep themselves occupied. And they used furs from the sea otters they had killed as money. Steller tried to stop them from killing so many of the otters, but the men would not listen. When winter was over, they built a small vessel from the remains of their ship. By the time these men left, they had killed nearly a thousand sea otters. The men took along as much sea otter meat and as many furs as they could carry. When they returned to Siberia, they sold the furs at high prices.

The next spring another expedition set out for Bering Island, and when it returned, it brought back thousands of sea otter, fox, and fur seal furs. The news spread, and the great fur hunt had begun. Hunters set out in boats of every size. Many people drowned making the dangerous journey, but many others returned with shiploads of furs.

Shipwrecked on a barren island in 1741, the Russian explorer Vitus Bering and his crew found sea otters resting on the beaches.

Fifteen years after Bering Island was discovered, the last of the sea otters had been killed there. Meanwhile, by 1745 the hunters had traveled east to the Aleutian Islands.

The Commander Islands had been uninhabited, but the Russians found people living on the Aleutian Islands. The native Aleuts were wearing long garments made of sea otter fur, which the Europeans named parkas.

The sea otters in the Aleutians did not come onto the shore as they had in the Commander Islands, and the Russians had a hard time hunting them. At first the Russian hunters traded with the Aleuts, who hunted the otters from special boats. But the greedy Russian hunters soon made slaves of the Aleuts. Women and children were held hostage—and they were killed when the Aleut hunters did not bring enough sea otter pelts.

The Russian hunters moved from island to island in the Aleutian chain as they wiped out the sea otters and other fur animals. They continued to use the same cruel practice of enslaving people in village after village. Twenty years after the fur hunt began, the Russians had crossed three quarters of the distance between Bering Island and Alaska. Not only did these Russian hunters drive the otters to near extinction wherever they went, but they also destroyed the Aleuts' culture. Many Aleuts were murdered. Diseases brought by the hunters killed many more. Finally, by the 1760s, the hunters had crossed over the Aleutian Islands and reached Alaska.

THE HUNT IN THE SOUTH

Spanish explorers sailed along the Pacific coast of Mexico and California and traded with the Native Americans before they colonized that part of America. At that time many sea otters could be found along the shore and on nearby islands. Sea otter pelts were purchased from the Native Americans and brought to the Orient to be traded. By 1800 the Spanish had sold more than ten thousand sea otter pelts.

In 1778 the sea otter hunt broadened to include many other nations besides Russia and Spain. Captain James Cook, the famous British explorer, was traveling in the Pacific Northwest, searching for the Northwest Passage, a shortcut to China. His two ships reached what is now Vancouver Island in British Columbia. The island people who met the ship were eager to trade with the explorers. Among the items these people offered were sea otter furs. Captain Cook's crewmen had seen sea otters all along the coast during their journey. They did not know that they were valuable but thought that these soft, warm furs would be useful for their trip north.

The explorers did not find the Northwest Passage—but when they stopped at a Chinese port on the way home, the sea otter furs they carried were noticed. Merchants quickly bought them at high prices. Later, when a book about Captain Cook's voyage was published in 1784, people began traveling from all over Europe and North America to trade with the people living along the Pacific coast for the valuable sea otter furs.

Meanwhile, the Russian hunting in Alaska and the Aleutians was placed under the control of a Russian fur company. To keep up with increasing demand, the Russians also traded with Native Americans in what are now the states of Washington, Oregon, and California. They teamed up with U.S. traders as well. The Russians sent Native American hunters down in U.S. ships to sneak along the Spanish-controlled California shores to kill sea otters. Sea otter furs were then called "soft gold" because they were considered so valuable. A single pelt could sell for as much as one thousand dollars—a fortune in the nineteenth century.

In the early 1800s there were about 150,000 sea otters living along the shore between Mexico and Alaska. The Russians founded a settlement in northern California called Fort Rus (which is now Fort Ross) as their headquarters in the south. In 1841 the Russians sold Fort Rus. But in the twenty-nine years that the Russians had control of the fort, their hunters killed fifty thousand California sea otters.

FORT ROSS — ФОРТ РОСС

The booming trade in otter furs led the Russians to
found a settlement, now Fort Ross, in California.

VANISHING SEA OTTERS

The great fur hunt ended slowly over time as sea otters became harder and harder to find. People no longer hunted them in the Aleutian Islands by 1808. By the 1830s the Russians had practically stopped searching for sea otter pelts. In 1867, Russia sold Alaska to the United States. But in the 126 years that Alaska and the Aleutian Islands were occupied by the Russians, it is estimated that they and many other nations killed about 800,000 northern sea otters.

When the United States purchased Alaska, the sea otters had not been hunted for several decades, and the population had recovered to more than 100,000. But many in the United States were quick to begin hunting them again—and by 1900 there were almost no sea otters left in the world.

FROM THE BRINK OF EXTINCTION

By the early 1900s more than one million sea otters may have been killed—900,000 northern sea otters and 100,000 to 200,000 southern sea otters. Sea otters were nearly extinct by 1911, when Russia, the United States, Japan, and England signed a fur treaty protecting sea otters and fur seals. Scientists believe there were only between 500 and 1,000 sea otters left then, scattered over a dozen isolated locations across their entire range. In 1913, President Woodrow Wilson made the fur treaty into U.S. law. However, poaching continued over the years, and by the 1920s sea otters had even disappeared from a few of these remaining locations.

Their number continued to decline until many wildlife experts were uncertain whether there were any sea otters left in the world. Then, in the 1930s, sea otters were discovered in the Aleutian Islands and in Prince William Sound in Alaska. A sea otter sanctuary was then set up on Amchitka Island, so that scientists could learn about sea otters and keep an eye on their numbers.

For a long time sea otters were thought to be extinct in California. In 1938, however, a California couple testing a telescope spotted a group of California sea otters off the coast near Big Sur. A sea otter refuge was

**Sections of the California coast have been set
aside to create a refuge for sea otters.**

established to protect these creatures. Then, as the otter population
slowly recovered, the refuge was extended further up and down the coast.

Protected by laws, sea otters in California and Alaska slowly began
recovering. By 1945 it was estimated that the world's sea otter population
had grown to about three thousand. But in the late 1940s, scientists found
that many sea otters were starving to death on Amchitka Island—there
was not enough food to support the number of otters living there.

RELOCATING OTTERS

Scientists decided to try to move some of the Amchitka Island otters to other areas in Alaska where otters were no longer present. In 1951, thirty-five sea otters were captured and moved, but they all died. Scientists tried again in 1954 and 1955—but again, all of the otters died. This was because scientists at that time did not understand much about sea otters and could not care for them properly. Many otters died because they did not groom themselves while being transported, and so their fur could not protect them from the cold. Some others died from overheating. And some died from digestive problems that developed during transportation. Because of all the problems, the relocation projects were abandoned.

Meanwhile, by the 1960s the population of southern sea otters had slowly increased, so that many people traveled to California to get a look at them. The public became much more aware of this marine mammal. Environmentalists saw the sea otters' story as proof that a species that was near extinction could make a comeback when it and its habitat were protected.

In 1965, the United States tested a nuclear bomb underground near Amchitka Island. An even larger explosion was scheduled for 1968. Environmental groups were upset because they feared that the sea otters in the area would be endangered. The U.S. Atomic Energy Commission agreed to move many of the sea otters to other areas before the second test.

Over the next seven years, state and federal agencies in the United States, as well as agencies in Canada, worked to move more than seven hundred sea otters to locations in Alaska, British Columbia, Washington, and Oregon.

Gradually scientists figured out the important factors necessary for safely capturing, transporting, and releasing sea otters to new locations. A transport crate was designed to supply all the sea otters' needs without injuring the creatures, for example.

Scientists also learned that sea otters need to become used to new surroundings before they are released. In 1970 an airplane load of sea otters from Alaska was flown to the coasts of Washington and Oregon. When they were released, the sea otters scattered in all directions. So, when another group of sea otters was released later that year, they were kept in holding pens in the sea before their release. These otters became more familiar with their new surroundings and stayed in the area.

Scientists are not sure exactly how successful the relocation programs of the 1960s and 1970s were. Sea otters can now be found in many areas along the Pacific coast in Alaska, British Columbia, and Washington. But whether these populations were formed from animals that were relocated there is not certain. Not many people live along the coastline in the remote areas where the sea otters are found. So it is possible that some of the otters living there today may be members of the original otter population that had survived the great fur hunt and had just not been noticed before.

Sea otters are doing much better in some areas than in others. Ninety-three sea otters were relocated to the Oregon coast in the early 1970s, for example, but only one was spotted in the early 1980s, and none have been seen since. Scientists are not sure why the sea otters did not survive in Oregon. Did they all die, or did many move to other areas?

Thanks to efforts to protect sea otters, they have made a remarkable recovery. Today sea otters can be found scattered over much of their original range. There are about two thousand sea otters off the California coast today, and their population has been growing by about 5 percent

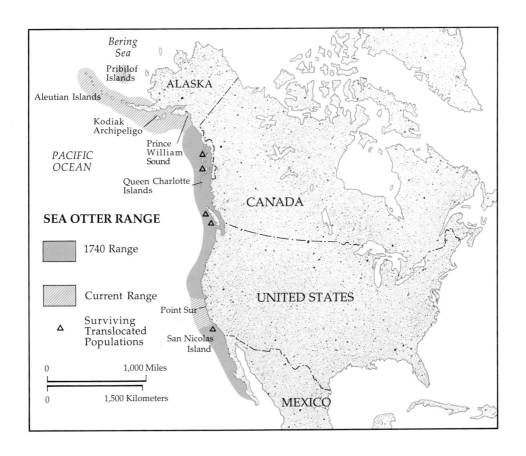

Bering
Sea

Pribilof
Islands

ALASKA

Aleutian Islands

Kodiak
Archipeligo

Prince
William
Sound

PACIFIC
OCEAN

Queen Charlotte
Islands

CANADA

SEA OTTER RANGE

1740 Range

Current Range

UNITED STATES

Point Sur

Surviving
Translocated
Populations

San Nicolas
Island

0   1,000 Miles

0   1,500 Kilometers

MEXICO

each year. The northern sea otters are further along in their comeback—
their current population is estimated at 100,000 to 150,000. However, as
sea otter numbers have increased, these sea mammals have come into
conflict with some people whose livelihood depends on fishing. Over the
last few decades this conflict has grown—and it has come to reflect a
much broader battle between those who wish only to use the environment and those who wish to protect it.

CONFLICT WITH PEOPLE

For fifty years, from the early 1900s to the 1960s, hunting sea otters was illegal. Poachers faced serious fines for killing or capturing the animals. Strict laws were very effective in helping the sea otters to recover. In the 1960s there were so many sea otters in Alaska that the state of Alaska allowed the hunting of one thousand otters. In the 1970s some Alaskans thought the otter population was large enough to permit limited hunting each year. In California people also wanted to be able to kill otters—not for their furs or meat, but because of conflicts between sea otters and fishermen.

FIGHTING OVER FOOD

Otters must eat a lot to survive. The average sea otter can eat as much as 9,000 pounds (more than 4,000 kilograms) of food each year. One of its favorite foods is abalone. Although it must use up a lot of energy to harvest this large sea animal, once the sea otter finds one, it doesn't have to gather as much other food. There may be 2½ pounds (about 1 kilogram) of meat in one abalone shell.

Humans also harvest abalone, both for food and for their pretty shells. But when sea otters move into an area, the number of abalone that humans can gather from that area decreases. (Abalone fishermen are allowed to harvest abalone only when they have reached a certain size. Sea otters not only compete for these large ones but also take many abalone that have not yet grown to the legal minimum.) Sea otters compete with fishermen for other types of food, too.

A diver harvests sea urchins. Parts of this animal, which is related to the starfish, are considered a delicacy in Japan.

There are, of course, two ways to look at the situation. You can say that sea otters are eating up shellfish that human harvesters need to make their living. Or you can say that human harvesters are taking from the ocean food that many marine animals, including sea otters, need to live. They have harvested millions of tons of seafood products from the Pacific Northwest each year. This isn't just excess food—the seafoods that people take out of the ocean are part of a complicated ecosystem that is being changed by human activities. Meanwhile, sea otters help to protect the kelp that feed and shelter many water animals.

Even though it is illegal, some fishermen have killed sea otters that have moved into their fishing grounds. Many fishermen are angry because regulations designed to protect sea otters and other marine mammals make it harder for them to make a living. In fact, many areas are now off limits for fishermen. There are also laws to regulate how they harvest fish. Over the years many marine mammals, including sea otters and porpoises, have died because they were trapped in nets used by fishermen. Now, laws in California limit the use of certain types of nets.

ARE WE OWNERS OR CARETAKERS OF NATURE?

The conflict between sea otters and the fishing industry is part of a much larger debate over the use of the environment. Some people feel that the needs of people come before the needs of animals. But others believe that humans have a responsibility to all the creatures that live in our world. Animals such as sea otters have adapted over millions of years to live in a particular environment. They don't have as many options about what to eat or where to live as people do. The fact that some people make a living harvesting shellfish is not a reason to get rid of the sea otters.

In the past, economic considerations almost always won out over concern for wildlife. But in the 1970s and 1980s conservation became an important national and international concern. From the beginning, sea otters were seen by the public as cute, interesting, and clever—so public sympathy has often been on the otters' side.

In 1973 the Endangered Species Act was passed. This major law, built on several earlier laws dating from 1900, provided protection for animals and plants in danger of becoming extinct. The California sea otter was listed as a "threatened" species in 1977. This means that it is protected under the Endangered Species Act because otherwise it could become endangered. The U.S. Marine Mammal Protection Act, which took effect in 1973, also provides protection for sea otters. Today, harming a California sea otter or other marine mammal can result in a fine of at least twenty thousand dollars.

WHY HELP SEA OTTERS?

While the debate continues, environmentalists are finding economic reasons to protect sea otters. One of these is the key role otters play in the health of the kelp forests. Many fish that are important to the fishing industry find shelter in these kelp forests. The kelp industry itself has also become a big business. Seaweed products are used to make ice cream, mayonnaise, toothpaste, car polish, and fingerpaints thicker and smoother. They are also used in making textiles, paper, and medicines.

There is also the fact that sea otters attract tourists to California shores, which brings business for many local hotels, restaurants, and gift shops. Tourists take boat trips to see sea otters and buy many souvenirs, such as otter T-shirts, stuffed animals, posters, and paintings.

Visitors to the Monterey Bay Aquarium in California are charmed by the sea otters there.

Public awareness is one of the most important factors in protecting endangered wildlife. When an endangered animal's struggle makes the news, people often work harder to protect that particular animal. This was certainly true for the sea otter. A group called Friends of the Sea Otter had a large part in helping the public become aware of the conflict between otters and people. The efforts of concerned people had helped the sea otter make a miraculous comeback from the brink of extinction, and efforts made by this group and other concerned people have helped to stabilize sea otter populations. But human activities still threaten the sea otter's future.

STILL IN DANGER

Competing with sea otters for food is not the only way that people threaten their survival. Many people use the California coasts for recreation, such as waterskiing and riding motorboats. When these activities take place too close to sea otter rafts, the animals may scatter and become distressed. Sea otters are very sensitive to stress—this is one of the major reasons these animals are hard to raise in captivity. Sea otters may also be injured by fast-moving boats or water skiers.

Pollution is one of the biggest dangers threatening all life on our planet. People have polluted the oceans in many ways, placing the lives of many different sea animals in danger. Sewage, industrial waste, and chemicals have been dumped into the oceans. Pesticides run off from farmlands into rivers, which empty into the sea.

Pollution in the ocean ultimately affects humans, because we eat animals and plants that live in the waters we pollute. But pollution has a much harsher effect on the animals that live in the water. Some pollutants can kill sea animals. Although pollutants have not been directly linked to any sea otter deaths, dead sea otters have been found with high levels of toxic chemicals in their bodies. Pollutants can affect all sea mammals indirectly. Smaller animals and plants absorb these poisons, which are stored in their bodies. As sea otters eat these sea animals and sip seawater containing bits of poisoned kelp, larger and larger doses of poisonous pollutants build up in their bodies. These chemicals can cause serious problems—for example, damaging the animal's reproductive system so that fewer new otters are born. Industrial wastes released into the water can also cause water temperatures to rise, which can be harmful to otters.

Oil spills are probably the biggest danger of all for sea otters. When a sea otter's coat is covered with oil, the fur becomes matted and no longer holds in a blanket of air bubbles. Then the otter cannot keep warm and may freeze to death. Even if it is able to clean the oil off its fur before it becomes chilled, its internal organs can become damaged because of the oil it swallowed while cleaning itself, or its eyes and lungs may be damaged by the oil fumes.

Huge oil tankers pass through the waters where most sea otters live. In March 1989, many seabirds and sea otters died when the tanker *Exxon Valdez* spilled oil into Prince William Sound in Alaska. The story of the *Exxon Valdez* oil spill is a perfect example of how people place animals like sea otters in danger. It is also an encouraging story about how people have helped animals in need.

OTTER RESCUE

In the late 1980s, ten to fifteen thousand otters lived peacefully along the rocky coast of Prince William Sound in Alaska. When the *Exxon Valdez* struck a reef in the sound, 11 million gallons (41.6 million liters) of poisonous crude oil spilled into the water. Severe weather conditions made it hard to control the oil spill; oil spread across 1,200 miles (about 1,900 kilometers) of coastline, making this the worst oil spill in U.S. history.

Animal rescue experts came from all across the nation to help save injured otters and birds. Hundreds of ordinary people—students, teachers, businesspeople, and homemakers—also volunteered their help. An otter rescue center was set up in Valdez, shortly after the oil spill. A second center was set up in Seward, Alaska, after the spill continued to spread. Rescuers worked long hours to clean and care for the otters.

Other people went out on boats looking for otters that had been soaked with oil. At first the animals were tracked down when they washed ashore. Later, more were captured in nets. The otters were placed in special crates, and rushed to the rescue centers in seaplanes and helicopters.

Animal rescue workers blow-dry a sea otter after oil from the *Exxon Valdez* spill has been cleaned from its fur.

At the rescue centers, otters were given tranquilizers to keep them from hurting themselves or rescuers. If an otter had swallowed a lot of oil, a mixture of water and activated charcoal was pumped into its stomach to absorb the poisonous oil and allow it to pass out of the animal's body.

Then the otter was brought to a washing room, where four people spent up to two hours washing and rinsing the animal's fur over and over until the oil was gone. Next the otter was towel dried and brought to a drying room where blowers were used to dry and fluff out its fur for another hour and a half.

Placed next in a recovery room, the otter was carefully watched. If it seemed to be all right, it was then placed into a tank of water. It was kept in the water for longer amounts of time, and was then taken to a larger tank where it could be with other otters. If the otter still seemed to be doing well, it was given antibiotics and flown to a large enclosed pen that was built in Little Jakolof Bay near Homer, Alaska.

Rescue scientists wanted to release the healthy otters in an oil-free area as soon as possible, but they were not sure how to go about it. Would the otters try to come back to their old homes, and in doing so become oiled again? The otters couldn't stay in the holding pens indefinitely. It was expensive to feed and care for them, and no one knew how long they would stay healthy under these conditions.

Twenty-one sea otters were released in the eastern part of Prince William Sound, which had not been affected by the spill. The otters had been implanted with a special tracking device so that scientists could keep track of them. They stayed in the area where they were released, so scientists knew that other healthy otters could be released there, too.

It is believed that as many as 3,000 to 5,000 otters eventually died because of the oil spill. But of the approximately 350 sea otters that were brought into the otter rescue centers, about 200 were saved in a rescue effort that went on for five months. The discouraging thing is that many of the otters that were returned to the wild died later. The knowledge that was gained, however, will make rescue efforts more effective in future emergencies.

PROTECTING CALIFORNIA SEA OTTERS

Northern sea otters are spread far enough apart that a single oil spill could not endanger all of them. But many people fear that a similar oil spill off the California coast could kill all of the southern sea otters. Some precau-

Other Otters Are in Danger, Too

THE NUMBERS of nearly every kind of otter in the world are decreasing. Giant otters, for example, were once found in many rivers in northern and central South America. Like the sea otter, the giant otter was overhunted for its fur. Riversides were cleared so that people could use the land for farms and villages. Mining and other industries polluted the rivers. Now only a few small populations of this otter are left.

Other endangered otters in South America are the marine otter of Chile and Peru (also called the sea cat) and the southern river otter of Argentina and Chile. The numbers of Eurasian otters are decreasing, too, in the rivers, lakes, and streams of Europe, Asia, the Middle East, and North Africa where they once thrived.

Once river otters were killed as pests. Now laws in many areas in Great Britain prevent them from being killed and protect the habitats in which they live. River otters are also counted regularly so that scientists know how well they are doing.

The Otter Trust, set up in England in the early 1970s, has raised and bred several kinds of river otters in captivity. The success of this group has allowed it to send otters into other breeding programs and to reintroduce otters into their natural habitats.

tions have been taken. So far, oil drilling has been prevented in the sea otters' range, for example. But oil tankers still travel close enough to the coast so that a spill could cause a catastrophe.

In 1987 the U.S. Fish and Wildlife Service began moving some southern sea otters to San Nicolas Island in Southern California to try to establish a second colony. By the early 1990s, 139 sea otters had been tagged and moved. However, many of the otters tried to return to their original homes. By early 1994 there were only 16 adults and 2 pups still on the island. Still, otter experts believe the colony is solidly established, although it will be a long time before its numbers increase.

Meanwhile, the USFWS is also attempting to keep otters out of areas where they might conflict with fishing and other human activities. But such otter control measures have had only limited success; the otters that have been removed from an area usually manage to get back in.

THE SEA OTTER'S FUTURE

People nearly drove the sea otter to extinction by overhunting. Then people helped save the sea otter by preventing hunting and setting aside protected habitats, so that it is no longer on the brink of extinction. But we have to be careful to make sure that we do not endanger them again.

FURTHER READING

Bailey, Jane H. *The Sea Otter's Struggle*. Chicago: Follett, 1973.

Bailey Jill. *Otter Rescue*. Austin, TX: Steck-Vaughn, 1992.

Chanin, Paul. *The Natural History of Otters*. New York: Facts On File, 1985.

Holyer, Ernie M. *The Southern Sea Otter*. Austin, TX: Steck-Vaughn, 1975.

León, Vicki. *A Raft of Sea Otters: An Affectionate Portrait*. San Luis Obispo, CA: Blake Publishing, 1987.

Paine, Stefani. *The World of the Sea Otter*. San Francisco: Sierra Club Books, 1993.

Smith, Roland. *Sea Otter Rescue: The Aftermath of an Oil Spill*. New York: Dutton, 1990.

Friends of the Sea Otter publishes magazines, *The Otter Raft* and *Otter Pup*.

ORGANIZATIONS

California Fish and Game Commission
P.O. Box 944209
Sacramento, CA 94244-2090
(915) 653-4899

Friends of the Sea Otter (FSO)
P.O. Box 221220
Carmel, CA 93922
(408) 373-2747

Sea Otter Center
(FSO educational/retail outlet)
Barnyard Shopping Center
Carmel Valley, CA 93924
(408) 625-3290

U.S. Fish and Wildlife Service
Department of the Interior
Washington, DC 20240
(202) 208-5634

Sea otters can be seen at marine aquariums along the Pacific coast, including:

Monterey Bay Aquarium
886 Cannery Road
Monterey, CA 93940
(408) 648-4800

Point Defiance Zoo and Aquarium
5400 N. Pearl Street
Tacoma, WA 98397
(206) 591-5335

Sea World
1720 S. Shores Road
San Diego, CA 92109
(619) 222-6363

Vancouver Aquarium
W. Georgia Avenue
Vancouver, BC, Canada
(604) 682-1118

FACTS ABOUT SEA OTTERS

Length	Males: a little more than 4 feet (1.2 meters) long; females: a little less (lengths include a 12-inch [30-centimeter] tail)
Weight	Southern: males average 65 pounds (30 kilograms); females 45 pounds (20 kilograms) Northern: males average 80 pounds (36 kilograms); females 60 pounds (27 kilograms)
Fur	Adults have velvety brown to almost black fur, lighter on the underside (older adults have a gray or white face); pups have woolly yellowish fur
Food	Abalone, sea urchins, clams, mussels, crabs, octopuses, squid, barnacles, snails, scallops, sea cucumbers, marine worms, starfish, limpets, chitons, sea anemones, fish, and other marine wildlife
Reproduction	Can breed every year starting at three or four years old, but may breed every other year; a female usually gives birth to a single pup
Care for young	Female takes care of the pup and keeps it with her constantly except when she dives for food

Range	Scattered populations in coastal waters along the Pacific coast, from California to Alaska to the Russian Commander Islands, the Kuril Islands, and the coast of Japan
Population size	About 2,000 southern (California) sea otters; estimated 100,000–150,000 northern sea otters
Social behavior	Live together in groups called rafts and are sociable but not truly social animals; do not interact very much and do not depend on each other for feeding, grooming, or defense; males and females have separate rafts and get together only briefly during courtship; do not form permanent mating bonds
Life span	15 to 20 years

INDEX

ABOUT THE AUTHORS

Alvin Silverstein is a
professor of biology at the
City University of New York,
College of Staten Island;
Virginia Silverstein, his wife,
is a translator of Russian scientific literature. Together they
have published nearly 100 books
on science and health topics.

Robert Silverstein joined his
parents' writing team in 1988
and has since co-authored more
than a dozen books with them,
including the Food Power nutrition
series from The Millbrook Press.